5/03

R0179076728

WILD BIRDS

by Joanne Ryder
illustrations by Susan Estelle Kwas

HarperCollins*Publishers*

Library of Congress Cataloging-in-Publication Data
Ryder, Joanne.
  Wild birds / by Joanne Ryder ; illustrated by Susan Estelle Kwas.
      p.   cm.
  Summary: The birds that glide through the sky, hop through the grass, and sing on the
fence gradually come to feed from a child's hand.
  ISBN 0-06-027738-6 — ISBN 0-06-027739-4 (lib. bdg.)
  1. Birds—Juvenile fiction.   [1. Birds—Fiction.]   I. Kwas, Susan Estelle, ill.   II. Title.
PZ10.3.R954 Wht   2003   99-042218
[E]—dc21   CIP
                                                                                       AC

Typography by Jeanne L. Hogle
1 2 3 4 5 6 7 8 9 10
❖
First Edition

For my parents, Dorothy and Raymond Ryder,
who always welcomed wild birds to our garden
—J.R.

For my sister, Mary
—S.E.K.

Wild birds glide from high

to low

lightly, brightly
speckling treetops.
They flicker
here and there
between leaf and leaf,
between earth and sky.

Wild birds
take the high path

over your head
under the clouds.

Wild birds dip
from sky to twig to earth,
hopping or walking,

tiptoeing through the grass.

Sometimes they stay
and share this yard,
this tree with you.

Wild birds swoop
at cats creeping
and dogs leaping
near their nests.

But stand away,
and you can spy
widemouthed babies
peeping for breakfast.

Wild birds sing
from rooftops and fences
and wires strung high.

They chirp before dawn
and fill your waking dreams
with song.

Carefree birds
bathe with a flurry of feathers,
splashing, spraying
puddle drops everywhere.

Chilly birds
puff into fat, fluffy balls
dotting the branches
at summer's end.

Then . . .
flyaway birds
sail across the moon,
leaving you behind
to watch the sky
and wish—

good-bye.

Stay-at-home birds
see their world
grow bleak and bare,
feel the wind
turn crisp and cold—
just like you.

Ever-so-patient birds
line the frosty branches,
waiting till they hear
the door creak,
your footsteps—
which they've come to know—

crunching in snow.

Ever-so-hungry birds
watch your shadow
slowly stretching
on the white ground.
They see you
fill the feeder
with sweet seeds,
then move away.

Wild birds,
swooping and looping,
flutter before you
as you stand
still as an icicle,
still as a frozen tree—
until a bold one
leaps
from the air
to you.

You are holding
a handful of feathers.
Small feet dance
on your mittens.
An eager beak plucks
seeds from your palm.
And you feel
a wild heart beating,
beating quickly—like yours.

With a leap,
she is gone.

With a leap,
someone new
dances on you,
on your cap-covered head.

And you feel

like a wild one too,

in the quiet cold,

so close to these

wild,

wild birds.